My Notes

Just A Family Who Loves Thanksgiving

My Notes

My Notes

Just A Family Who Loves Thanksgiving

My Notes

My Notes

Just A Family Who Loves Thanksgiving

My Notes

My Notes

Just A Family Who Loves Thanksgiving

My Notes

My Notes

Just A Family Who Loves Thanksgiving

My Notes

My Notes

Just A Family Who Loves Thanksgiving

My Notes

My Notes

Just A Family Who Loves Thanksgiving

My Notes

My Notes

Just A Family Who Loves Thanksgiving

My Notes

My Notes

Just A Family Who Loves Thanksgiving

My Notes

My Notes

Just A Family Who Loves Thanksgiving

My Notes

My Notes

Just A Family Who Loves Thanksgiving

My Notes

My Notes

Just A Family Who Loves Thanksgiving

My Notes

My Notes

Just A Family Who Loves Thanksgiving

My Notes

My Notes

Just A Family Who Loves Thanksgiving

My Notes

My Notes

Just A Family Who Loves Thanksgiving

My Notes

My Notes

Just A Family Who Loves Thanksgiving

My Notes

My Notes

Just A Family Who Loves Thanksgiving

My Notes

My Notes

Just A Family Who Loves Thanksgiving

My Notes

My Notes

Just A Family Who Loves Thanksgiving

My Notes

My Notes

Just A Family Who Loves Thanksgiving

My Notes

My Notes

Just A Family Who Loves Thanksgiving

My Notes

My Notes

Just A Family Who Loves Thanksgiving

My Notes

My Notes

Just A Family Who Loves Thanksgiving

My Notes

My Notes

Just A Family Who Loves Thanksgiving

My Notes

My Notes

Just A Family Who Loves Thanksgiving

My Notes

My Notes

Just A Family Who Loves Thanksgiving

My Notes

My Notes

Just A Family Who Loves Thanksgiving

My Notes

My Notes

Just A Family Who Loves Thanksgiving

My Notes

My Notes

Just A Family Who Loves Thanksgiving

My Notes

My Notes

Just A Family Who Loves Thanksgiving

My Notes

My Notes

Just A Family Who Loves Thanksgiving

My Notes

My Notes

Just A Family Who Loves Thanksgiving

My Notes

My Notes

Just A Family Who Loves Thanksgiving

My Notes

My Notes

My Notes

My Notes

My Notes

My Notes

Just A Family Who Loves Thanksgiving

My Notes

My Notes

Just A Family Who Loves Thanksgiving

My Notes

My Notes

Just A Family Who Loves Thanksgiving

My Notes

My Notes

Just A Family Who Loves Thanksgiving

My Notes

My Notes

Just A Family Who Loves Thanksgiving

My Notes

My Notes

Just A Family Who Loves Thanksgiving

My Notes

My Notes

Just A Family Who Loves Thanksgiving

My Notes

My Notes

Just A Family Who Loves Thanksgiving

My Notes

My Notes

Just A Family Who Loves Thanksgiving

My Notes

My Notes

Just A Family Who Loves Thanksgiving

My Notes

My Notes

Just A Family Who Loves Thanksgiving

My Notes

My Notes

Just A Family Who Loves Thanksgiving

My Notes

My Notes

Just A Family Who Loves Thanksgiving

My Notes

My Notes

Just A Family Who Loves Thanksgiving

My Notes

My Notes

Just A Family Who Loves Thanksgiving

My Notes

My Notes

Just A Family Who Loves Thanksgiving

My Notes

My Notes

Just A Family Who Loves Thanksgiving

My Notes

My Notes

Just A Family Who Loves Thanksgiving

My Notes

My Notes

Just A Family Who Loves Thanksgiving

My Notes

My Notes

Just A Family Who Loves Thanksgiving

My Notes

My Notes

Just A Family Who Loves Thanksgiving

My Notes

My Notes

Just A Family Who Loves Thanksgiving

My Notes

My Notes

Just A Family Who Loves Thanksgiving

My Notes

My Notes

Just A Family Who Loves Thanksgiving

My Notes

My Notes

Just A Family Who Loves Thanksgiving

My Notes

www.ingramcontent.com/pod-product-compliance
Lightning Source LLC
LaVergne TN
LVHW060328080526
838202LV00053B/4437